Mr. McDoogle's Dune Buggy Trip

Written and Illustrated By:
Marie Whitton

**For My Husband
Greg**

**For My Children
Gregory, Ann-Marie &
Kimberly**

**For My
Grandchildren**

What a beautiful day for a Dune
Buggy trip,
Mr. McDoogle did say "Let her rip"
Are there any secrets in this quiet
desert of the Southwest?
It will be the best.
Have to explore this wonderful land,
With all this hot and dry sand.

The desert is so vast and wide,
Sun beats hot - don't want to get fried.
Have to prepare for this trip.
Bring lots of water to sip.

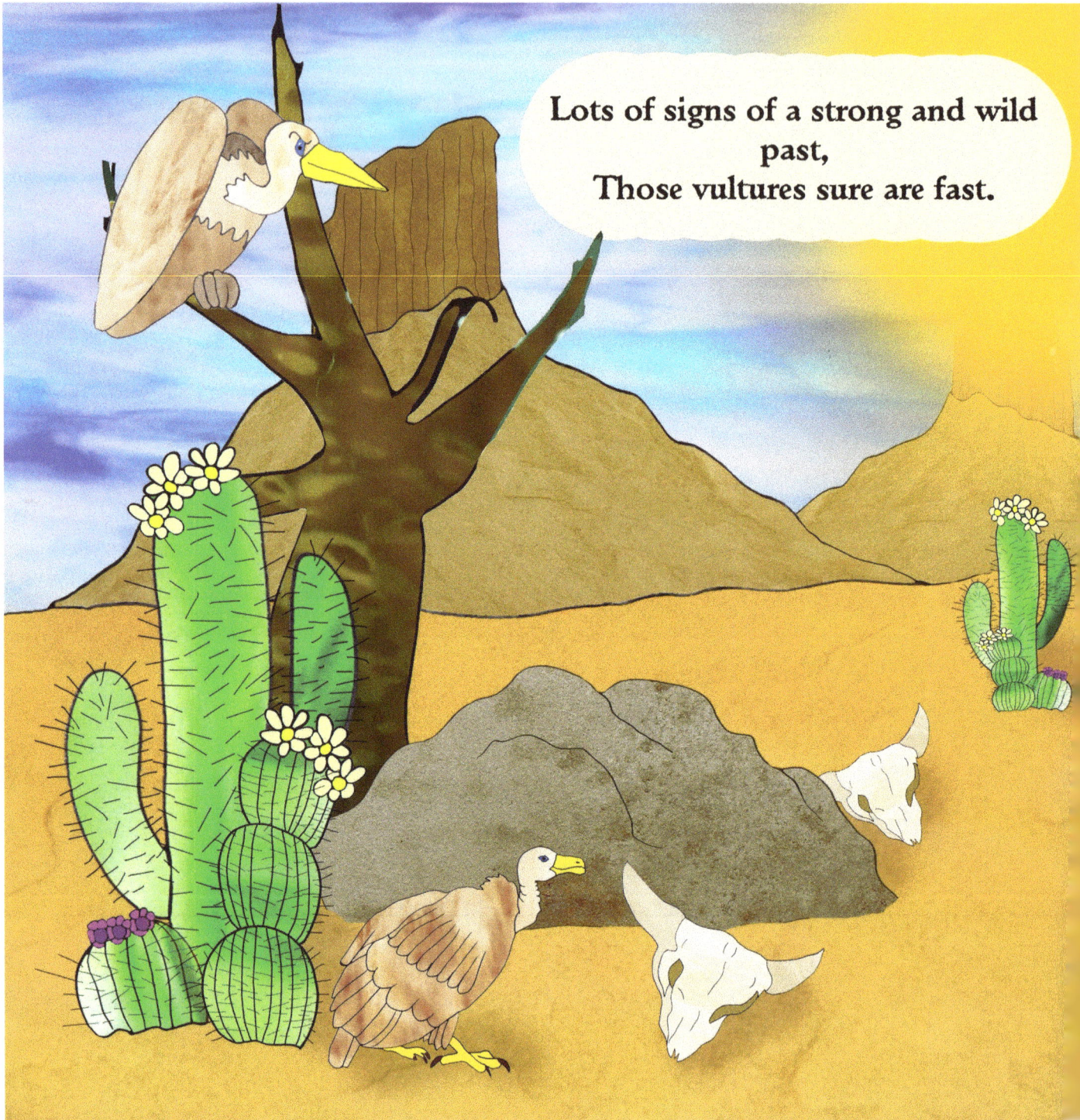

Lots of signs of a strong and wild past,
Those vultures sure are fast.

Looking over these old skeleton bones,
Are vultures humming there special tones.
They are looking to be fed,
Before they settle down and go to bed.

Look what Mr. McDoogle is seeing,
Prairie dogs are going to be fleeing.
With their noses high in the air,
Checking out if all is fair.

Mr. McDoogle -
What is that - behind the cactus?

The hawks and owls are on the prowl,
Hungry - they are looking for fowl.
He sees fleeing Road Runners and Quail,
He will be taking home this tale.

Around the next dune he spots all kinds of snake,

From the Dune Buggy- a picture - Mr. McDoogle will have to take.

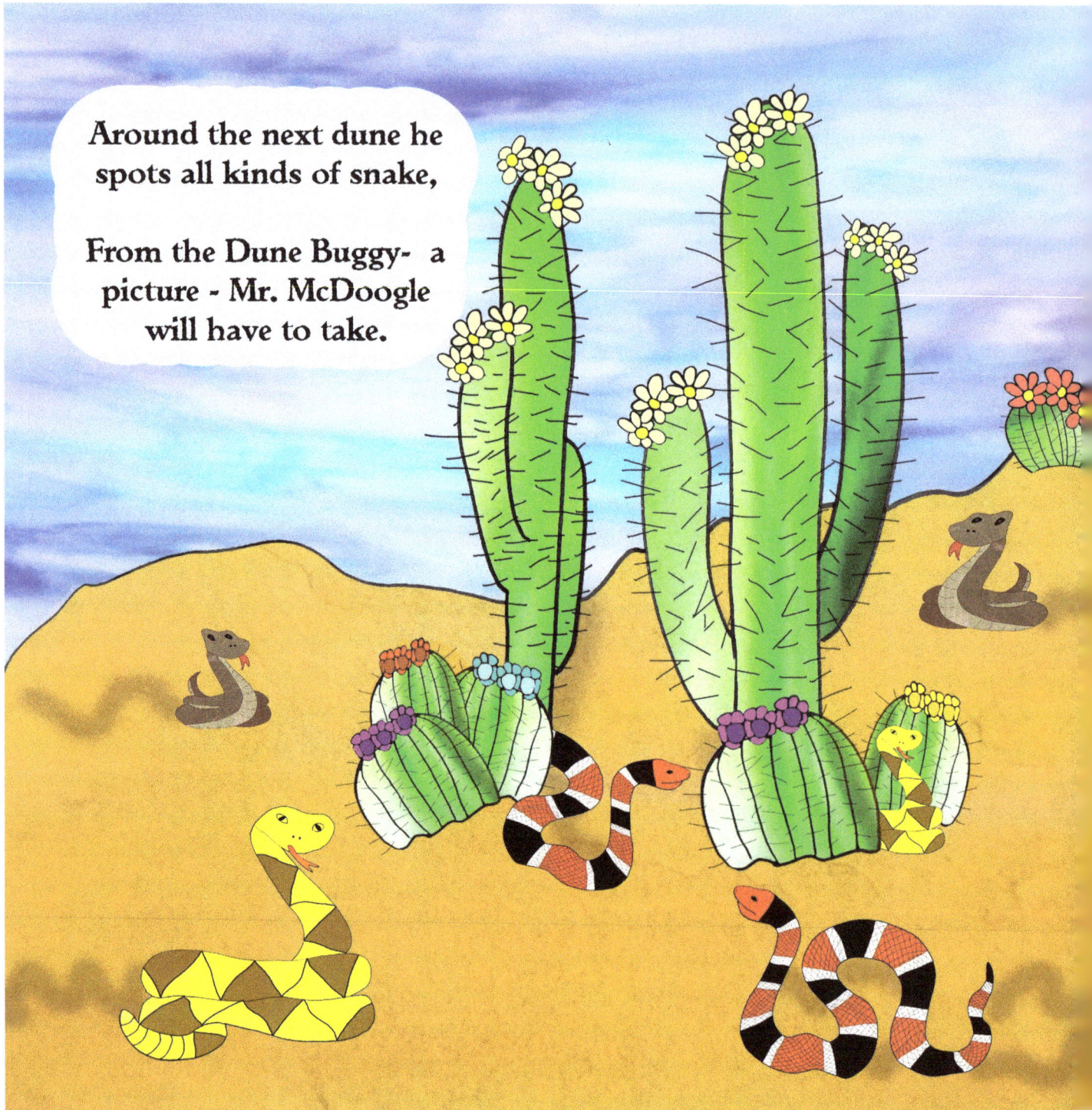

There are sidewinders and rattlers and coral,

All slithering through and around the cactus floral.

Desert, to live, is a tough place,
Not many people make it their base.
To stay here - you have to be strong,
You need to be respectful or things will go wrong.

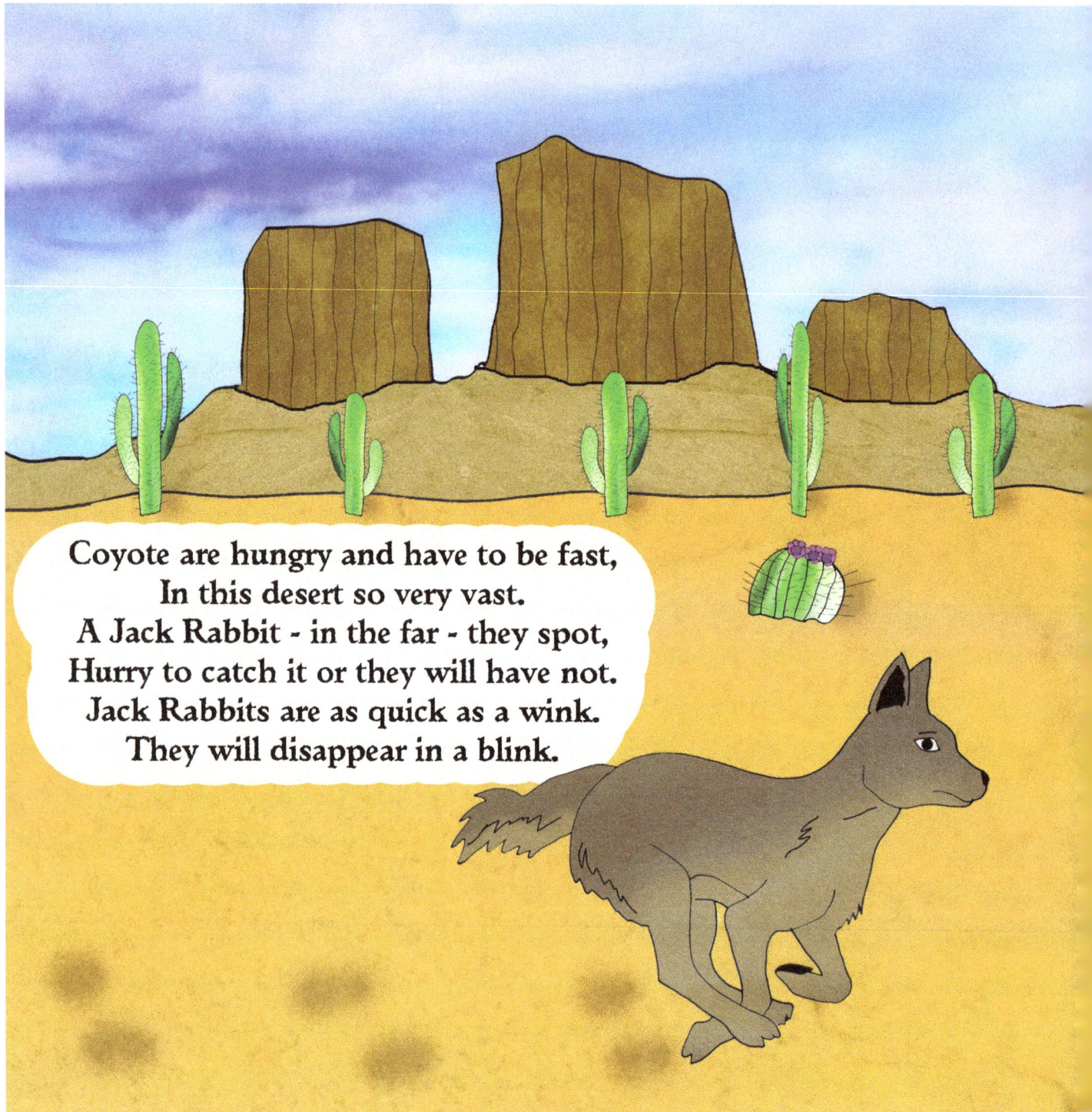

Coyote are hungry and have to be fast,
In this desert so very vast.
A Jack Rabbit - in the far - they spot,
Hurry to catch it or they will have not.
Jack Rabbits are as quick as a wink.
They will disappear in a blink.

Be careful not to fall into the Mountain
Lion's path.
Or they will see his wrath.
To the Ringtail Cat - they will pass,
They will keep running until they run
out of gas.

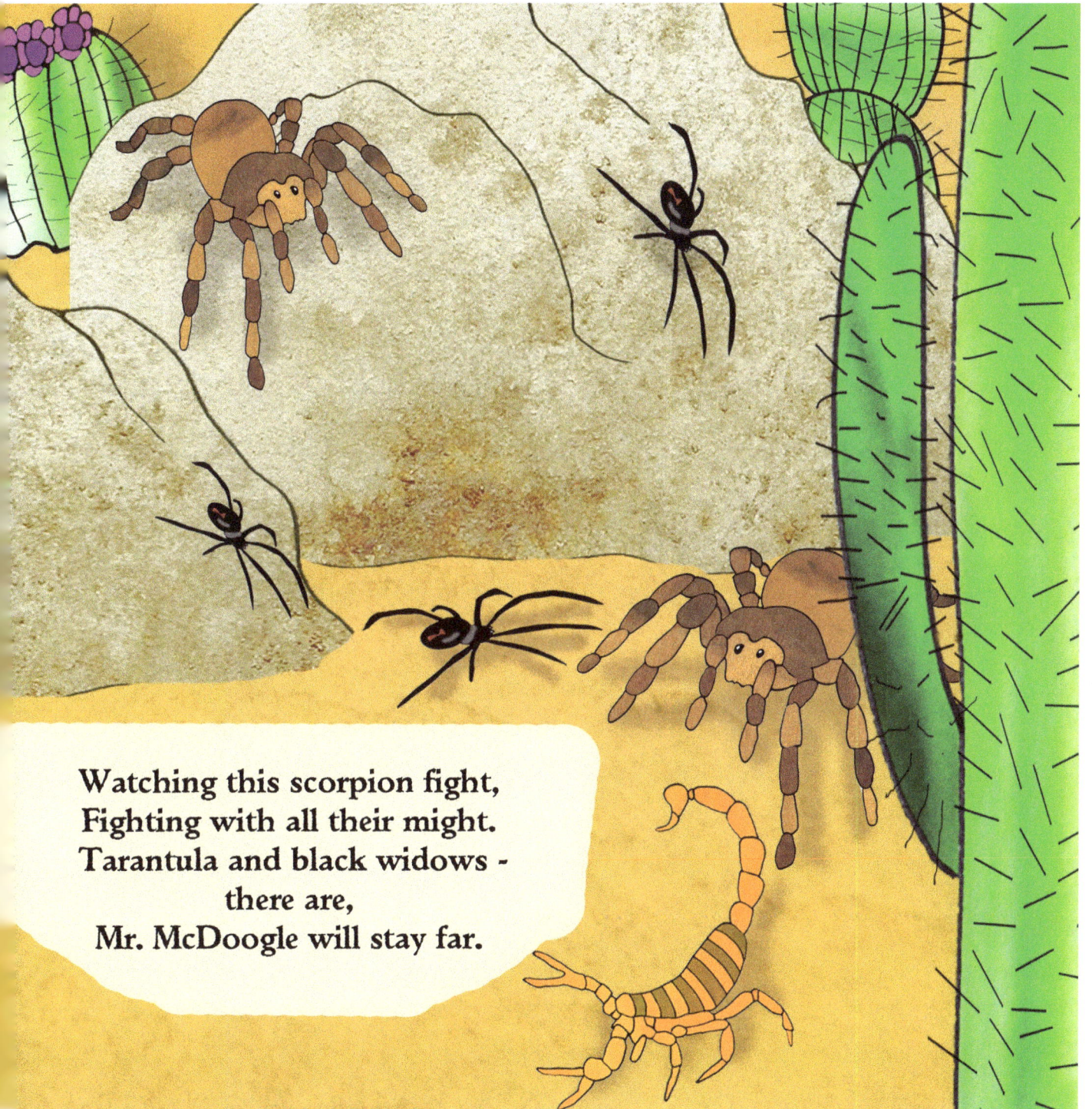

Watching this scorpion fight,
Fighting with all their might.
Tarantula and black widows -
there are,
Mr. McDoogle will stay far.

Over here behind these rocks -
what does Mr. McDoogle find,
Reptiles of all kind.
There are Gila monsters and Horned Toad,
It is time to go, look for more and travel the road.

Around the corner - Mr. McDoogle smells
a familiar smell.
A smell that he knows so very well.
Be careful and stay out of the way,
Or those skunks will spray.

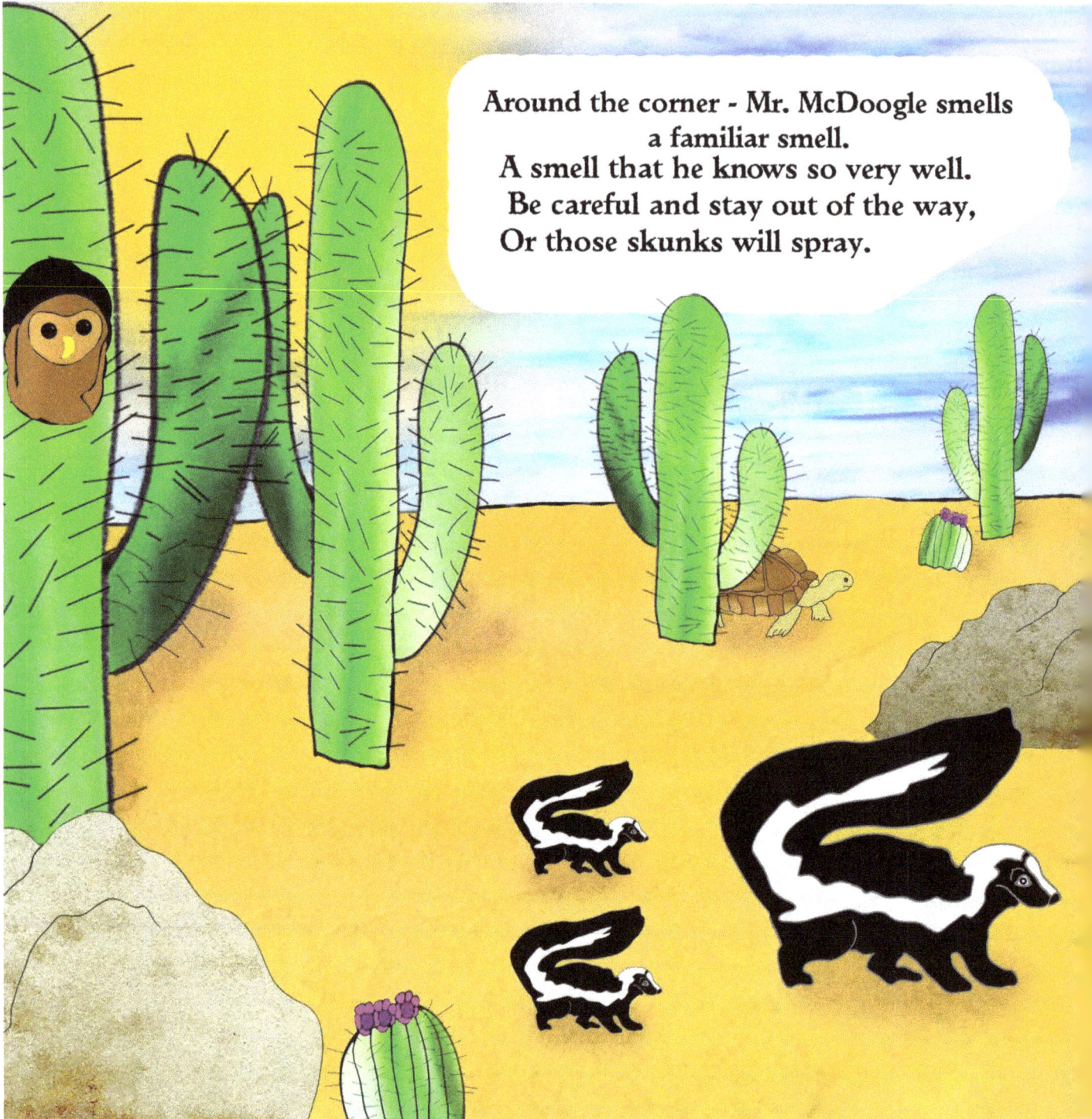

The hawks and owls are again on the prowl,
This time there is no fowl.
They are after kangaroo mice.
Oh, how nice.

There are secrets in the desert of the Southwest,
It was the best.
Lots of life in this quiet place,
All existing in their grace.
What a wonderful time Mr. McDoogle had,
Leaving for home with memories - he is glad.

www.ingramcontent.com/pod-product-compliance
Lightning Source LLC
Chambersburg PA
CBHW060754150426
42811CB00058B/1408